"The poems in *The Apple of Their Throat* make my queer heart do so many things: sink, shimmer, do a little jig. I read them and I'm reminded of what happens when we, as Norman writes, 'let grief sing'—when we allow ourselves to open, to make art—we find each other. We realize, sometimes in the pages of a book, we were never, and are never, alone. I want to give this book to every queer kid hiding in the back pew, trying not to be seen. Kevin T. Norman sees you."

— **GRANT CHEMIDLIN**
author of *In the Middle of a Better World*

"Poems that plant hope deep in my chest! Kevin uses the alchemy of poetry to evangelize the queer experience into delicious fruit, no longer forbidden."

— **JOE SANTINI**
author of *Inside the Riptide*

"Poems that feel like you're seen through words. In life, in love, in loss, and in growing pains. Words that perfectly bring emotions you can't even begin to describe. Who should read this book? Every single person who's ever felt they didn't possess the love they seek out."

— **DEAN LIN**
Creator, Host, Motivational Speaker

the apple of their throat

poems

kevin t. norman

2026

This book is a work of creative expression. Although it draws upon the author's personal experiences, it includes fictionalized elements, alterations, and composite characters for literary effect. As such, it should not be read as a literal or factual account. Any resemblance to actual persons, living or dead, or to actual events is purely coincidental or used in a fictionalized manner.

Published by Central Avenue Poetry, an imprint of Central Avenue Marketing Ltd.
centralavenuepublishing.com

THE APPLE OF THEIR THROAT: Poems

978-1-77168-461-3 (pbk)
978-1-77168-462-0 (ebk)

Printed in United States of America

1. POETRY / LGBTQ+ 2. POETRY / Subjects & Themes - Religious

1 3 5 7 9 10 8 6 4 2

To the one still hiding,
it's okay to come out now.

“You must not eat fruit from the tree
that is in the middle of the garden,
and you must not touch it,
or you will die.”

— Genesis 3:3

I

POLLINATION

The irony is not lost on me
that fruit led to sin, and that is now what they call people
like me.

The first time I kissed a boy
we hid in his bedroom

closet pretending to play
hide-and-seek.

My hands touching the future
of my body through the puberty of his.

Fingers sticky
with his pleasure,

and his empty
from the lack of mine.

The world demanded
a sacrifice. So I ripped

myself

open, let grief sing
a melody, and that is how
I discovered poetry.

We're meeting tonight at seven if you're free.

I was, but I didn't know anything
about God other than I wasn't allowed
to love him and be who I wanted
to be. I was 18,

and although the world considered me
an adult, they told me I was still a child
in his eyes. If that's true,
then maybe it was safe to not know

the difference between the Old and New Testaments,
or how to pray. And even now I know
I am not what they consider holy
but maybe it's not too late for me

to still grow up to be.

Christ, sanctify me.
save me.
embolden me.
wash me.
strengthen me.
hear me.
hide me.

From the evil
call me
to you,
with your Saints

Amen.

I am jealous of our clothes on
Sunday morning. How they sin
so openly, brushing against one another
when we fidget while we sit.

Interlocking
in their own quiet prayer
begging me loudly to bend
my knees
in worship.

I always knew
I was gay.

I just didn't always know
I was allowed to be.

My mother wouldn't look at me
when I told her I might be gay.

Her open love quickly closed
into a clenched fist. It wasn't anger,

but rather fear playing dress-up
in its oversized clothes.

And in one breath, I no longer fit
within the inherited frame of picture-perfect.

Painted myself outside the lines
with every color I could find

inside the box. A black sheep now
dipped in rainbow, and suddenly

she was unable to bear the weight
of a word I'd carried

on my shoulders for over twenty
years. Maybe this is why I slouch.

Struggle to put my shoulders back
because some days I am still afraid

of a word that makes everyone afraid
of me.

I grew up being told I could be anything
I wanted, but when I chose
to be authentically myself

suddenly anything forgot to grow

up with me.

You told me that your standard
of love was the start. *If it worked*
with us then it will be safe
for you. But, why can't I
be the hero in the story? The one
who has the chance to show you
how the world could be
spun. Instead I find
new ways to let you shine.
A closed mouth here.
A smile over there.
So I watch your stories and rewrite them
in my head. Wishing
for only one episode in the season.
It's art you learn to make
at an early age
when you are the only whisper in a crowd
-ed room.

The night we met I had 3 shots
of vodka with nothing
but the desire to meet you

to chase it.

I am terrified of making a mistake
of us. Of my trembling hands

holding on too tight and   letting go
too soon. I never learned how to measure

without doubt. Taught to give a whole heart
but in pieces, a smile with less teeth.

What I mean is, how can I make you
want to stay with someone

who is still learning
who he needs   to be?

What made you think of your parents?

you asked, glancing over at me from the driver's side. We had just left the beach on our first date, and it crashed into me like a lifetime. This was the moment I discovered love didn't operate within time. Because the way your eyes held mine, how my name curved along the crooked frame of your smile, and your hands licked the salt of my skin left an imprint in a home I built for love. And when asked if you believed in it you took my faith and offered doubt. So I knew at that moment, I could no longer tell you I thought of my parents because they made me believe in us. The reason I saw tomorrow wrapped in today and how my dad knew the night he met my mom she was the woman he would marry. Instead I just pointed through smudged glass at a nearby restaurant and lied, telling you that was their favorite place to eat.

We have seven more minutes
trapped inside this closet.
Wool coats tickle our necks

as we choke
down the hot, damp air
our nerves mold between us.

Tomorrow you will say
you were drunk, and this was a dare
you never meant to play.

I will be too stubborn to admit that
that will hurt me. But still, we lie
inside with an open-mouthed kiss.

And through our parted lips,
I plant infertile hope
inside the hollow of your chest.

Pray that love can grow
in deserts. Battling to understand
why this is always the only way

I can reach you.
Inside closets,
at the bottom of an empty glass.

We are like the ocean and the shore.
We ebb
          and flow
between holding on
                    and letting go,
anxiously awaiting the continuous crash
                              and its aftermath.

Dance with me
until the music dies.

Dance with me
even if they turn
the lights back on.

The moments I crave
are when silence speaks what only hearts can

feel. When it fills the page
where our words should be

and our eyes become open
mouths and our bodies conjugate

like language.

Where are the words to describe how I feel
about you? It's too soon to call it love,

too late to say crush, and far too beautiful
for lust. Each day is a countdown until you leave

back to your corner of the Earth,
but I was lucky enough to witness my first miracle

as God bent the planet in half for our lips
to meet. Maybe there are no other words for this

moment. No one will ever understand
the inner workings of a miracle so I won't try

and seek past what I can see,
because for once maybe love can be

this simple.

In the beginning,
exploring my sexuality

felt like I was traveling
far away from myself.

Now, it feels as though
I am coming home.

All I can remember is the sweat
dripping down our skin
loosening up the friction

between moral and immoral, and this feeling
is what I wanted. The freedom to tuck myself
into sheets without the shame

of *who* or *how* or *why.*
There was power in my choice
to bring him home.

Sex didn't have to carry meaning.
It could be two drunken, lonely strangers

free-falling

through liquor-stained dance floors
and bar doors onto cracked sidewalks.
Plummeting into bed in a tornado of torn-off clothes

and rushed decisions.
Room spinning, heart racing, face flushing
while everything we touched grew

with the smell of sweat and vodka.

After we had sex
I watched as he folded himself
back into an apology. The one I memorized

for those guilty nights
when I needed to pray
for a straighter tomorrow.

Soon our conversations became scriptures.
The bedroom became a sacrifice.
And all I could do was   wait

three days until Lazarus decided
to resurrect what he prayed
would just stay dead.

How could I ever believe
in a god that wants us
to be anything other than who we are
in love?

I like to think that when Eve ate
the fruit she knew
exactly what she was doing.

Boldly stated, *Fuck him,*
and took another
juicy bite.

He wasn't the best kisser
but he was the one

I wanted to kiss.
It was the first time I ever felt my body

crave someone and want to touch them.
I made him more holy

than the religion we hid ourselves in.
The one that told us hands were made

for prayer and not each other,
but still, we used them in worship.

And that is how I found God.
Discovered love under the bed

-sheets and his body. All the places we were
preached never to look. I made a home

in what they call sin,
and never had I felt more holy.

Our lips crushed kisses into wine
and I got drunk
on the possibility of forever.

I am jealous of a piano
because of how your fingers tease
their keys. I want to be
the only thing that sings
when you touch them.

Is there a way to describe this feeling?
How every day feels like sinking

deeper into what looks like love,
even though you are not here

to hold, or here to breathe
onto me *good morning.*

But I awake to dreams of drowning
in you. Suffocating through memories

of what has been while floating
through the hope of what could be.

And despite the life we still have
left to live in between,

my only hope is that
somehow it's lived with you

and me.

Gay bars taught me more about love
than churches ever did.

Because inside that rainbow
neon glow and on those sticky floors

I could be every part of myself
I was taught not to like

and no one demanded I sacrifice
it to be anything else.

You smell like burnt marshmallows
and chocolate on a summer night.

Travel stamps the passport of your skin,
and now my hands
have
a braille
of memories
to be read
across your spine.
I find adventure in the crooks
of your body. Along the mountain range

of your shoulders and up the current
of your thighs. You unfold a world

inside a bed frame. Offer a lifetime in your palm
and I would give anything to forever

be a part of that.

I won't dull
this rainbow
inside to shine
only in one color.

I didn't come out in a parade
of flashing colors. There was no buildup.
No rehearsed monologue in my bathroom

mirror. I didn't shout it loud
-ly.   Slipped away from the church
like the sound of an unanswered prayer.

I ate the apple of men's throats in bars
I wasn't old enough to drink in.
Found love while   fumbling

through the dark for the light
switch, and when I turned it on,
watched as everyone   scurried.

The church fed me
poison one sermon
at a time and called
it healing.

You taught me the anatomy
of our bodies and I learned
how to fall in love.

Being gay sometimes requires silence.
This, I call survival.

Whether for safety or fear,
we often don't show

who we are. How sometimes I call him
friend, and how he doesn't

confess to the drunk girl at the bar flirting
with him that we're more

than casual. People don't realize
what a mutiny it is to hold

his hand in a crowded room.
Or how our kiss could slash religions

apart. I wonder if it will
always be like this,

small lies stored like white stones
in pockets. With each moment spent

further from the truth, and both of us
shuffling closer to the deep end.

I'm afraid to love because I've loved.
And looking at you reminds me

of everything I want,
everything I've lost,

and absolutely everything
I want to hold on to.

If religion is simply about surrendering
our demons you are my favorite
one.

When we were kids
our mom would break
our toys when she was angry.

Smash them into pieces and blame
my brothers and me
for the wreckage. Now I know

it was more than just emotion,
but back then I thought
it was how all parents treated misbehaving

children. I misunderstood
the moments when it was more
than an object.

When my mother would crack
her stone-faced shell open,
darkness and light blended inside

the fractures. Michelangelo once said
he saw an angel
in the marble and carved

until he set him free.
And now I believe my mother
was always trying

to do the exact same thing.

I wish I had known
sooner that the closet
I was locked in
unlocked from the inside.

No matter how many times I tell myself
my heart will never know the difference
between you and love.

Masculinity was a ghost inside a chapel.
An echo in a hollow body.
It was the day in 11th grade
when the crack of my voice whipped against a room
full of testosterone and body spray. It hid
in the hands of boys with footballs and a scoreboard.
Something people in a crowd would spend a night cheering for.

Masculinity was bookmarked in the voices of proud parents,
I just know when he grows up he is going to be a ladies' man.
It was a letter labeled: return to sender. A report card
with no grades.

Masculinity was the sleepovers I was never invited to.
The parties where teenage hearts dared and lips kissed truths
with the spin of a bottle. It was a winning prom,
a laurel of plastic, and the loss of childhood
in the backseat of your dad's old car.

Masculinity was a dream never awoken. A promise made
and broken with a twist
of a limp wrist. It was a meal ordered
but never eaten.

Masculinity was a prayer
left unanswered, and the answer
to cure what they called

me.

Put a pen in my hand and I will write you
a world. Poetry is alchemy
and every word a substitute
for *I love you*.

And I will preserve us.
Keep hope safely inside the glass
walls of these poems.
Allowing fear close enough to see

but far enough away to never touch.

I sometimes wonder if the stars look down
and think we are the ones who are shining,
and if they make a wish each time we fall

in love.

You let me plan our wedding before we were even a couple. Warm summer air bled through the holes in my jeans as I sat drunkenly sprawled against a brick wall outside the Satellite. Cell phones the red string connecting Los Angeles to Australia, and tonight I tugged at the lifeline. You soberly confessed you didn't want a wedding, only a marriage, and I slurred through that with words like a hammer and told you how I always wanted one. Shattered truth floated in silence across the Pacific and suddenly I wanted to drown in another drink. But you threw me a life raft in the shape of a promise and said,

Then I would have a wedding.

And when drunken words gave birth to sober thoughts, my heart finally heard yours whisper, *I do.*

2.

FERTILIZATION

There once lived a poet
who convinced the god of death to bring his love back
to life, and that is why I still write
you poetry.

The beginning of the end
of the world looked like a first date.

It cracked in quiet hope
and eager surrender. It was soft

as a compliment and jaded as a thought
wrapped in gray jeans and a blue henley T-shirt.

The end of the world smelled
of cigarettes and burned

like spearmint. It held love
in promise and surrendered

with dimple-cheeked smiles.
It was a mistake

revealed in goodbye,
and a lesson learned

in time.

Is this what love feels like?
A chair with two legs.

A meal without a napkin.
What I mean is:

is love meant to feel like a pop
quiz? A cucumber when you expected a pickle.

Is love supposed to hurt like growing
pains? Invisible and necessary

for tomorrow. Because I thought
love was the rainbow

after a storm. A dessert
when you swore you were full.

I thought love would heal
instead of hurt. And somehow this ache is all you

left and I have no words
that describe what you called love.

The breakup was a dance
I didn't learn the choreography

to. I never heard the music
start but you picked the song.

Turned my body until I was spiraling
towards an exit. Trudging on

two left feet until goodbye
cut in and ushered me

through the rest of the dance
home.

The truth hid in the mundane
of things and I never thought to look.

Because you always left the toothpaste
cap on the other side of the shower.

Proving to me that you did not care
if two things were meant to be together

if it was more convenient
to be a p a r t.

Your phone was the snake.
His texts were the fruit.
I was the naive one
who went looking
for the truth.

My mom taught me how to close the door
between me and myself.

Through a sister dead
when Grandma died.

A childhood in Olivia.
Stitch-lipped and a jar of peanut butter.

She taught me it's not safe
to trust tomorrow,

and time taught us
the sharpest words are never spoken.

And so I learned to hide
from the rescue team.

And trust is now a whisper
in a stadium.

A weed in an arboretum.
A prayer under sheets

in a twin bed.
Asking God to let me find my way

back home.

When we broke up I spent a week
in my bed. Hid under the covers

and pretended the world was only
the size of my sheets. I didn't go to work,

and I never told them why. I slept
for days, only waking to go

pee. I learned that stomachs can
be an earthquake in an empty room.

Nothing inside to break but still unsettled.
Trapped you in poems

like a dog-ear between pages.
Saying, *This is where I can pick*

our story back up when I am done
crying.

My nephew once told me
that if I still loved you,
I had to tell you. But I didn't
understand how to explain
to him that sometimes people can hide
a dictionary in the back
of their throat and still have
nothing left to say.

I don't know how to move
on without packing you up
with me. That is why I drop
                                        you

in conversations. Say your name
so habitually it begins to taste sour
on my tongue.

It's like spelling a word and looking at it
too long. Second-guessing
if letters are supposed to look like that.

I want to wear you out.
Or down. Whichever means the weight of you
will no longer be what I call heavy.

I know we are a dead thing. But
I will continue to expel you
from the depths of my lungs

until I can find another reason
worth breathing.

If love is a language
you spoke in the present tense
I spoke in **future**
and now we're only left to *the past.*

I am insecure about my body.
The way it hangs on my bones. Loose
and stretchy in all the *wrong* places.

Once, you laughed
at the lines that snaked across
my skin. Asking how someone so young

could stretch and demand so much
space. As if it were a crime to love
myself to the point of spilling

over. So I began to eat
less. Wore clothes too big.
I had never found a reason to hate

the size of my body
until the day you asked
me why I didn't.

If you don't like the way I write
about the grief why did you leave
me so much of it?

I still write about us
because this is my version

of a photograph. I need something
to look back on and point to

when there is crushing grief
and say,

See, here in this stanza,
we were happy once.

Our hearts are cracking
and love is slowly sinking.
Fault lines are forming
through our promises

and now all I wish
is that we were a car
crash. I want our breaking
to be quick.

Crashing in the middle
of a song still so far from the ending.
But instead I can spot the finish
line. Watch as love flakes

away like the blue paint inside
your bathroom. And here we are
two captains slowly going down
with the ship.

If there is a gentle way for a heart
to break I have yet to find it.

Space has new meaning between us
when you're no longer in it.
Suddenly it is not miles,
or airplanes, or missed calls

and goodnights.
It is standing in a house
party two shots deep laughing
with friends and feeling complete

-ly alone. It's knowing that tomorrow
the sun will rise but everything will still
be dark. Space feels small
when you have a bridge to cross

it but no one has answers when it crumbles.
We are told time fixes all wounds,
but how much time
does time need to mend

what I have left of us?

I will allow myself to feel
every piece of this heartbreak
because it is all that I have
left of you.

We spoke the same
language but in two different fonts.
Mine elongated and yours compressed

to fit a Post-it note.
Always sticking exactly
where you wanted yourself to be.

I loved the way your lips left
their color on my body
and how your teeth

tore into the thinnest parts of my skin.
I loved how goodbye gave birth
to hope and how hello welcomed

love back in.
It made similarities feel different
and routine something new.

And most of all I loved
how I loved when it was you.
But I loved

and I loved
and I loved
until there was no one left to love

but me.

Note to self:

stop flirting with disaster
and calling the pain love.

Questions I don't want answered

I often wonder if you're happy.
Not that I believe you deserve it.

Not that I believe anything
about you, but I do wonder

when I look at the pictures of you
two what exists behind his smile.

Does he ache when you don't
pick up the phone? Do you have someone

behind the scenes pulling the strings
to your hunger? Does he think

your heart is only for him,
and is it only for him?

Did you ever think of me
after you said goodbye?

Do you ever think of me
now?

The T-shirt you gave me to remember

the first night we met
hangs in my closet only

to be worn by time
and plastic. There's a sun stain

on the front because I left it
too long in my car with your note

still attached to it. I think I kept it
in there because I wanted to feel

like you were still here. Moving
with me, not across oceans.

But in all the years I have had your shirt
I have never tried it on. I like the question

of us a lot more than the answer
to whether or not we fit.

The truth is,
we will get over this
love, and our promise
of forever will make
a liar out of you
and me.

Little kids talk about the strangest things,
or maybe I forgot how to live
in my imagination. I think

I can only be creative if I have a drink
stronger than how hard love could hit
me. Tonight, it is sparkling

wine so I can remember the wiggle of caterpillars
in my stomach, or as my nephew would say,
on my tongue. Because sometimes words change

their meaning after they fly
out of our mouths. Like how your *goodbye*
meant *forever*, and all the ways in which I let it.

When I told my nephew I had a broken heart
he put his small hands on my chest and pushed
them together. *There,* he said, *now it isn't*

broken. And just like that,
we both believed
in magic.

I am an architect in the way I can plan a future.
I built you a freedom within my words
and it's here you break
me while they build
me back
up.

I'm sorry I'm sorry I'm sorry I'm sorry I'm sorry I'm sorry I'm sorry I'm sorry I'm sorry I'm
sorry I'm sorry I'm sorry I'm sorry I'm sorry I'm sorry I'm sorry I'm sorry I'm sorry I'm sorry
I'm sorry I'm sorry I'm sorry I'm sorry I'm sorry I'm sorry I'm sorry I'm sorry I'm sorry I'm
sorry I'm sorry I'm sorry I'm sorry I'm sorry I'm sorry I'm sorry I'm sorry I'm sorry I'm sorry
I'm sorry I'm sorry I'm sorry I'm sorry I'm sorry I'm sorry I'm sorry I'm sorry I'm sorry I'm
sorry I'm sorry I'm sorry I'm sorry I'm sorry I'm sorry I'm sorry I'm sorry I'm sorry I'm sorry
I'm sorry I'm sorry I'm sorry I'm sorry I'm sorry I'm sorry I'm sorry I'm sorry I'm sorry I'm
sorry I'm sorry I'm sorry I'm sorry I'm sorry I'm sorry I'm sorry I'm sorry I'm sorry I'm sorry
I'm sorry I'm sorry I'm sorry I'm sorry I'm sorry I'm sorry I'm sorry I'm sorry I'm sorry I'm
sorry I'm sorry I'm sorry I'm sorry I'm sorry I'm sorry I'm sorry I'm sorry I'm sorry I'm sorry
I'm sorry I'm sorry I'm sorry I'm sorry I'm sorry I'm sorry I'm sorry I'm sorry I'm sorry I'm
sorry I'm sorry I'm sorry I'm sorry I'm sorry I'm sorry I'm sorry I'm sorry I'm sorry I'm sorry
I'm sorry I'm sorry I'm sorry I'm sorry I'm sorry I'm sorry I'm sorry I'm sorry I'm sorry I'm
sorry I'm sorry I'm sorry I'm sorry I'm sorry I'm sorry I'm sorry I'm sorry I'm sorry I'm sorry
I'm sorry I'm sorry I'm sorry I'm sorry I'm sorry I'm sorry I'm sorry I'm sorry I'm sorry I'm
sorry I'm sorry I'm sorry I'm sorry I'm sorry I'm sorry I'm sorry I'm sorry I'm sorry I'm sorry
I'm sorry I'm sorry I'm sorry I'm sorry I'm sorry I'm sorry I'm sorry I'm sorry I'm sorry I'm
sorry I'm sorry I'm sorry I'm sorry I'm sorry I'm sorry I'm sorry I'm sorry I'm sorry I'm sorry
I'm sorry I'm sorry I'm sorry I'm sorry I'm sorry I'm sorry I'm sorry I'm sorry I'm sorry I'm
sorry I'm sorry I'm sorry I'm sorry I'm sorry I'm sorry I'm sorry I'm sorry I'm sorry I'm sorry
I'm sorry I'm sorry I'm sorry I'm sorry I'm sorry I'm sorry I'm sorry I'm sorry I'm sorry
I'm sorry **These poems are the apologies you never gave me.** I'm sorry
I'm sorry I'm sorry I'm sorry I'm sorry I'm sorry I'm sorry I'm sorry I'm sorry I'm sorry I'm
sorry I'm sorry I'm sorry I'm sorry I'm sorry I'm sorry I'm sorry I'm sorry I'm sorry I'm sorry
I'm sorry I'm sorry I'm sorry I'm sorry I'm sorry I'm sorry I'm sorry I'm sorry I'm sorry I'm
sorry I'm sorry I'm sorry I'm sorry I'm sorry I'm sorry I'm sorry I'm sorry I'm sorry I'm sorry
I'm sorry I'm sorry I'm sorry I'm sorry I'm sorry I'm sorry I'm sorry I'm sorry I'm sorry I'm
sorry I'm sorry I'm sorry I'm sorry I'm sorry I'm sorry I'm sorry I'm sorry I'm sorry I'm sorry
I'm sorry I'm sorry I'm sorry I'm sorry I'm sorry I'm sorry I'm sorry I'm sorry I'm sorry I'm
sorry I'm sorry I'm sorry I'm sorry I'm sorry I'm sorry I'm sorry I'm sorry I'm sorry I'm sorry
I'm sorry I'm sorry I'm sorry I'm sorry I'm sorry I'm sorry I'm sorry I'm sorry I'm sorry I'm
sorry I'm sorry I'm sorry I'm sorry I'm sorry I'm sorry I'm sorry I'm sorry I'm sorry I'm sorry
I'm sorry I'm sorry I'm sorry I'm sorry I'm sorry I'm sorry I'm sorry I'm sorry I'm sorry I'm
sorry I'm sorry I'm sorry I'm sorry I'm sorry I'm sorry I'm sorry I'm sorry I'm sorry I'm sorry
I'm sorry I'm sorry I'm sorry I'm sorry I'm sorry I'm sorry I'm sorry I'm sorry I'm sorry I'm
sorry I'm sorry I'm sorry I'm sorry I'm sorry I'm sorry I'm sorry I'm sorry I'm sorry I'm sorry
I'm sorry I'm sorry I'm sorry I'm sorry I'm sorry I'm sorry I'm sorry I'm sorry I'm sorry I'm
sorry I'm sorry I'm sorry I'm sorry I'm sorry I'm sorry I'm sorry I'm sorry I'm sorry I'm sorry
I'm sorry I'm sorry I'm sorry I'm sorry I'm sorry I'm sorry I'm sorry I'm sorry I'm sorry I'm
sorry I'm sorry I'm sorry I'm sorry I'm sorry I'm sorry I'm sorry I'm sorry I'm sorry I'm sorry
I'm sorry I'm sorry I'm sorry I'm sorry I'm sorry I'm sorry I'm sorry I'm sorry I'm sorry I'm
sorry I'm sorry I'm sorry I'm sorry I'm sorry I'm sorry I'm sorry I'm sorry I'm sorry I'm sorry

People often ask me,
Why are some of your poems so sad?

And I always reply,
So I don't have to be.

I blamed him for my
u
n
r
a
v
e
l
i
n
g
because it was easier than accepting
that my own two hands helped
unstitch myself. And in the end,
I was the one who closed
my eyes and jumped

whether or not he was
the one who convinced me
of the possibility of flying.

The Prayer:
Father,
be done;
on earth as in heaven.
And lead us not

Amen.

I continued to love God
long after I was told he didn't
love me. This became a new form of grieving.

A shedding of identity that I built
a shelter inside of and lived. Losing
him felt like rejection on your wedding

day. A blindside when the person you trust
most decides you are not worth saving.
They say to love another person

is to see the face of God, and I watched
as those I love twisted
their faces in disgust,

fear and confusion.
I thought breaking would be cracked
wood, sharp and loud

in all the worst places.
But it was quiet.
It looked like busy schedules

and unread messages. And silence
taught me that when you show
people who you are, you lose

who you were. And when they quoted
scripture to tell me all the ways my thinking
was bent and off course,

I quoted it back with Ecclesiastes 7:13,
Accept the way God does things,
for who can straighten what he has made crooked?

If memory is a time machine mine gets stuck in 2017.
My heart beating the dashboard
of my chest
looking for the kill switch.
But I know there is nothing
to shut down and yet
the body still remembers
what the mind can choose
to forget.

It is 2025 and you still forgot
to say goodbye.
Turned your back into a sail
and rode the ripples of my trembling
heart home. Tied stones to our story
in the Pacific and threw us
overboard.

And now I wonder
if you remember what my body is
still learning it's allowed
to forget.

Grief is love
learning how to say
goodbye.

3.

RIPENING

All I have known about fixing people
is that I have always had to break
to do it.

This is what healing looks like

- unpacked luggage
- refusing to get out of bed
- not showing up to work
- half-written poems on receipts
- a referral to a therapist
- uncontrollable crying in traffic
- googling how to build a time machine
- visiting the therapist
- replaying goodbye until the pages rip
- losing your job
- looking at photos of love moving on
- accepting you can't make a time machine
- laughing and not feeling guilty about it
- waking up and thinking of only breakfast
- going on bad first dates
- a goodnight kiss
- interlocked eyes across a restaurant
- a number written on a receipt
- a finished poem.

My mom once told me
while I was crying
that I would look back
on this heartbreak and laugh,
but I never believed her.

Tonight we served his name
across the dinner table
and again the tears came,
but this time they were swallowed
in all of our laughter.

He knows what's next
is nothing and so do I.
Still, we stretch these last minutes

together into dialogue. Asking
in every way except
directly if the other will stay.

But we tuck away our desires
with hands inside pockets and hearts dangling
from our sleeves. And at this moment I am thankful

for gravity. Because right now time is the only thing
moving. And if we keep talking I can pretend
we never have to.

I will call this war
the battle between my heart
and you holding it.

Maybe I romanticize too much
and our locked eyes are just a stare.

The blush of my cheeks too much
sun. My shaking body from the coffee

not electricity in your touch. Maybe
your words are conversation and not a poem.

Your smile not a secret and mine not the key.

On our third date you asked
me if I would ever write you poetry

but I have never written a happy poem
so I told you you had to break my heart

if you ever wanted these types of words
from me. You then looked at me

defiantly

and said, *Well then,*
I guess I hate poetry.

Archer pointed towards his wall
and showed me how to frame the heartbreak. To let it   hang
like a fishhook, something tempting
and a reminder of the freedom from being nearly caught.

I cried about him inside the bedroom before we took our clothes off.
Stripped his hands from my throat and threw them
on the carpet. Peeled his name from my lips and folded it
to try on again tomorrow.

Sanded down our story
until it was a stanza.
And let him help me spill ink
all over our ending.

I don't write poems
to say it gets better.
I write poems because
this is the only way
I think it does.

I need you to know
I am not perfect.
Actually, what I mean to say is

please remember that
I will make mistakes.
I am trying and learning

and I swear,

I am sorry if my growth hurts
you. Believe me when I say it hurts
me too. But like shaved hair

I will come back strong
-er, thicker, more determined
to stay rooted

to my body. That is a promise
I can keep. That is a promise
I believe is worth staying for.

They didn't lie when they said time heals
all wounds. Yet that doesn't mean they don't
scar. A remnant of a memory that once hurt

you. But scars are wounds that learned
to close. Proof of a strength I doubted
my body could carry.

And now, when I look at the marks
that still linger from his touch,
I think only of my hands that healed them.

I want to skateboard the Venice boardwalk
during a lavender-clouded winter sunset.

Take sharp turns through crowds
of tourists who think my home

is still worth visiting even in the cold
-est months. Throw our bodies into sand

-castles and crown myself the king
of the dunes. This will be a highlight

of my twenties. Along with the glass
plates, cups, and leftover bottles

of beer we catapulted at stone walls
after every college heartbreak. I want

to remember how fun it was to be kids
trapped inside our grown-up bodies.

In an alternate reality

There was no closet.
The words "coming out"
only asked by the neighborhood
boys when they wanted me to join
them in climbing the roof of the church
across the street. Turning the parking lot
into a communion of truth
or dare. A battlefield
of branch swords and wounded soldiers
in a baptism of mulberries.
Cory kissed me
beneath the bleachers after football practice.
I cheered for his games and lost
my virginity on a blanket in the field. Making love
into grass-stained memories. I never learned how to write
a poem. Fruit did not transform
into jam on a page and slip
into confessions. I don't pull my hand away
when he reaches out
to hold it. We don't have to practice contortionism
inside every room we enter and our bedroom
is no longer the only altar for love
-s resurrection. We break bread
inside the glass church by the sea
on our wedding day. And no one
has to call their life sin
just so they can finally be loved
and forgiven.

I can't turn my heart
back into a match
when we already started
this fire. So I will let myself burn
and I'll never apologize
for everything that comes
along with it.

What would happen if I let myself be happy?
That is to say, what would happen if there was not fear
on the stovetop of my stomach bubbling
to a boil. If I could write about us without subtext?

Paint inside the lines. Overindulge without having to throw up.
But love has always been a losing game
of hide-and-seek and I am afraid I will always be
it. But with you it feels like I am searching

in an empty room with the lights on.
Hunting for an answer when no one asked
a question. Yelling in the middle of a library
or fishing in a pothole. What I mean is,

I no longer have to be afraid
of goodbye. Of porcelain promises and love
like a blinking headlight.
I wonder what would happen if I let myself
be.

I worry that you are whole
while I am still only half
a person because I thought
love said we had to be half
of someone else.

I don't believe in God anymore

Except when I am on airplanes or driving a car.
Except when I am walking on the sidewalk near a busy intersection.
Except when I can see stars beyond the city lights.
Except when I am outside.
Except when I am eating food that makes my taste buds dance.
Except when I wake up in the morning.
Except when I watch my cat sleep in my arms.
Except when I read books or write poetry.
Except when I am surrounded by my friends.
Except when I am dancing on memory-stained floors.
Except when I pray.
Except when I kiss a boy.
Except when I drown in your island eyes.
Except when I have you.

Love will always be
right no matter how
many times we get it
wrong.

I don't think I ever let myself be angry.
Instead I shrink-wrapped sadness
loosely around my skin.
A makeshift bandage of gauze
and plastic that I thought hid
the bruising that his absence kicked
into me. I never told him
to *fuck off* because I cannot be cruel
to the things I love. Even if they don't love me
back. I let him disappear
like the hope before a sob. Fast and quiet
before the damage. I am angry I was not angry
and now there is nothing left
to let my rage run like a flood.
Healing became a drought
in order to grow new life,
and through the chapped, cracked earth
of my smiles, something new sprouted.
There was no anger in our death but enough
tears to grow something that looked nothing like us.
And my god, is it beautiful.

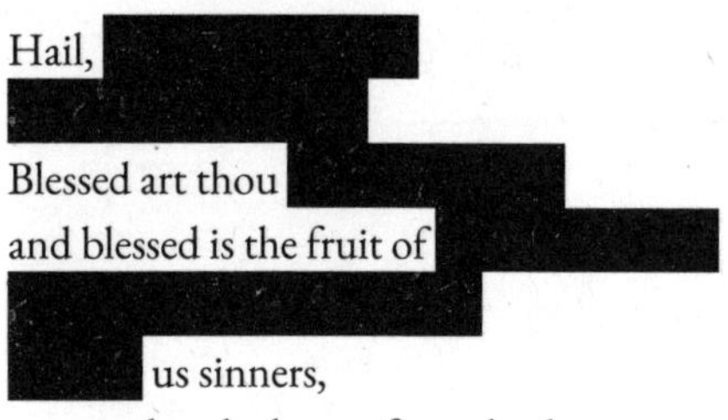

Hail,

Blessed art thou
and blessed is the fruit of

us sinners,
now and at the hour of our death.
Amen.

Come sit with me and let's forget
about tomorrow. Let's wrap ourselves
in coffee, books, and a television
binge. Fill our bellies with laughter

and every snack we can carry
because we refuse to pay
the extra ten cents to buy a bag.
Let me tell you how the color of your eyes

makes me want to write my favorite poem.
Then watch me write it. I want you to witness
my favorite way to make love.
This way whenever I am distant and lost

in the pages of a notebook
you'll understand I am never far.
Only out searching for new ways
to say I love you.

When I met you I didn't realize
you were the love poets wrote about.
So I pushed you away. Tried to locate the exit

in all your welcome signs.
I described your smile as mischievous
because I thought all good intentions paved the way

to hell. But you knocked on all of my locked doors
and when I refused to open them
you showed up outside with a boom box

and my favorite song.

Forgiveness is allowing my heart
to accept everything he's ever done
because it all led me to you.

There is no sweeter honey
than your blue-eyed
good morning. A creak

of the bed. The rainfall of our
shower. The daily news sneaks
through door cracks

from mini speakers.
Routine is the sound
of I love you. It means someone chose

to choose your chaos. Orbit in you
-r space and fall within you
-r gravity. This is what shooting stars

were made for. Or of. Or wished
on. Whatever the hell means dreams
come true. We are two objects in motion

that keep a world moving,
and we sound like an orchestra. The splash
of the water. The tug of a sheet. The shuffle

of feet. I will memorize the lyrics
of this morning's routine. Hum along
through the afternoon and sing

them as a lullaby to sleep. Repeatedly,
until the band kicks up and plays
it all again tomorrow.

The poets got it wrong.
Poetry doesn't need to be a string

of adjectives sewn together with pretty words.
Similes and metaphors. Poetry is you

and me on a sofa too small
for our limbs while crammed together

watching *Survivor* and eating
fig jam grilled cheese sandwiches.

I was looking for you
but I was not ready to find you.
You came unexpectedly
like an onion ring hidden in my fries.
Secretly wanted and with big surprise.

Like a party with all your friends
when you swore you only wanted a birthday at home
alone. I know if I had met you
any earlier we would not have today.
A house and a cat and six years

under our feet like a step
ladder helping us reach
tomorrow. I broke in
so many ways to learn
what it meant to feel. And now I am

feeling. Call me a pair of hands.
Call this life a dream. Something fragile
that I am afraid to break
so I try not to hold on
too tight. But I know you will

catch me. A net underneath the tricks
I learned to fly.
Never afraid of me letting go
because if I do you already know
how to catch me.

To all the boys who taught me
how to stay, I'm sorry
I left.

You keep rearranging the furniture
in our apartment and I don't know
if this is your way of playing hard to get.

A constant chase as I navigate new ways
to find old things. It is now a challenge
to find the cups when I want water.

It took weeks for my hands to understand
that the paper towels were now above
the sink. Every day seems to be a reminder

of my needing to reach back
into the past. Maybe I have grown
this way because everything around me

is constantly shifting. Phantom limbs grasping
shadows of memories I am still learning
to let go of. I no longer know where to draw

the finish line. I have spent my whole heart chasing
happiness and now that I've finally found it
all I want to do is stop

moving.

I don't know if you understand me.
I get lost in metaphors and imagery

because I can't help but craft
poetic ways to explain how

or why I might love you.
I can compare you to the sky

and say that being with you reminds me
of Icarus and the sun. I guess

it's all dramatic but we fall in love
with movie magic for the theatrics

and if you get lost among these metaphors
and adjectives remember that

at the end they always find their way
back to you.

Our lips are poets
and a kiss
their poetry.

If the priest were to ask,
I would confess everything
about us and ask for forgiveness
for absolutely none of it.

I don't understand why Happiness doesn't know
how to write a poem. Maybe because it's too busy
living rather than mourning what died.

Or it never learned how to spell
a laugh. I think Happiness doesn't know
how to write a poem because Happiness understands

how to sing in the quiet.
And even though the words don't flow
on paper doesn't mean they are not etched

into my skin. Inside my cheeks
when you enter a room
or the cold hardwood floor

under our bare feet. Happiness is a roommate
I never want to move out.
And even though Happiness can't write a poem

it does know how to feel them.

I finally stopped chasing
and decided to plant roots
in who I am. Just like flowers
I don't need to go searching
for hands to prove I'm beautiful.

Some days I will love you
and not know how to
say it. These are the days I wash

your egg-crusted pan or make the bed
our sleep disrupts. These are the days I watch
you instead of the movie or buy you yellow

roses because they remind me of my grandma
and how much I wish she had met you.
These are the days I won't pick up

a pen and write a poem. Because I don't know
how to compress a smile into a page.
I don't know how to express a feeling

worth more than words. So I'll pack a bag
and follow you across the sea.
Through the mountains. Down a beach.

On a trail. These are the days
my questioning mind won't force open
my mouth to ask, *Where are we*

going? Because it doesn't matter.
Chasing you is a thrilling adventure,
and I will blindly follow every twist

and turn of it.

I won't write you a love poem
on Valentine's Day. Because
I think they're cliché. Because
it's what I'm supposed to do

and I despise being told what to do.
Even by you. But mainly because
I don't need to be told to love
you. I simply love you.

Except not as much on Valentine's Day.
Because you're more than a holiday.
You're there on average days.
During my all-week Monday blues

or stuck-in-the-middle Wednesdays.
You're there when there is no reason
to celebrate. Which makes me want to celebrate.
You're the pre-New Year's Eve champagne

kiss the year we couldn't have our own.
You're the poems I'm still trying to write.
The ones I think about every time
we're in the same room.

But they won't be today.
Because we are worth more
than one love poem
on Valentine's Day.

An ode to my apostles

A lot of myself didn't make sense
but you saw the miracles
beneath my poems and chose to stay
long enough to see what they became.

Whether in a breakup
or in death. Distance or in time.
I will never be ready

to lose you.
I know everything must end
but that doesn't mean I want it

to. And I look at you sitting there.
Smiling shirtless with sticky, sweat-
covered skin. And we are both miserably hot

in this L.A. summer heat,
but I wouldn't want to be anywhere
else than slowly melting inside this apartment

with you.

It's time to go. And although I'm not
ready, you ask me to pack

up our worries and stuff them
between our yesterdays. Fold tomorrow

into our sleeves like hearts. And I know love
might not last forever, but it's alive

today. Here on a bench in a city
where language trips our tongues.

When what we want to say always falls
a little flat. But in the breaths between

I catch your eyes for reassurance. A trust
fall. Silently asking you to remind me

of the space we take and if it's okay
to take it. And while you hold my hand

on this hill, you point out
at the city and say,

In all of this, I was able to find
you.

If there is a heaven I don't want it.
Keep me here
sinning
and still calling it
love.

The world did not end with fruit.
It's how all of our stories began.

ACKNOWLEDGMENTS

Thank you for going on this journey with me. I hope that somewhere within these pages, something in you healed, broke open, or recognized the universality of love. You are never alone. If you've ever wrestled with your religion, sexuality, family, or self, know that this book (and I) are here with you.

To all the queer writers who came before me, thank you for paving the way. When I was coming out, I leaned on queer stories to guide me. You showed me that there is a world for us, even if we have to write it into being ourselves.

Michelle, Beau, Jess, Molly, and the entire Central Avenue team, thank you for the love and care you poured into this book. Each of you helped make it stronger in your own way. Michelle, thank you for opening the door when my persistence kept knocking. It means the world to see these poems finally find their home.

Andrew, thank you for believing in my voice when I couldn't, and for being the spotlight that illuminated every stage I've stood on. I wish you could see how far we've come.

Michael, my sassy gay best friend, I miss you every day. You helped me survive heartbreak and taught me to turn pain into art. Thank you for your unwavering support and for loving the roughest versions of these poems. I wish you were here to see that we made it.

To my friends and family, thank you for your constant encouragement, even when I looked like a wandering artist. Mom and Dad, thank you for every ounce of faith, time, and help you invested in me and my wild dreams. I know how rare it is for queer kids to have the support of their family, and I carry that blessing with deep gratitude. Jonathan, thank you for seeing the light in me and cheering for every way I let it shine, from poems to auditions. We're making dreams come true.

To my love, Daniel, thank you for letting me be wholly myself. You are the first man to show me what love can truly look like, and I'm so grateful for the life we're building together. You arrived as unexpectedly as these poems and became the balm that healed what once hurt. Thank you for giving me the safety to grow. I love you.

To my heart, Darrow: pspspspspspsps.

Kevin T. Norman is a queer writer and content creator based in Los Angeles, California. Followed by over 425,000 across TikTok and Instagram, he redefines what it means to tell stories in both the digital and literary worlds. He is the founder of Violetear Books, an imprint under Bindery devoted to publishing bold, marginalized voices. Kevin's poetry and creative vision have led to partnerships with Spotify, Amazon, Wattpad, and more. In 2022, he was honored as a TikTok LGBTQ+ Trailblazer for his advocacy in the digital space. He lives in Los Angeles with his partner, Dan, and their beloved cat, Darrow. *The Apple of Their Throat* is his debut collection.

Find him at @kevintnorman